The
Trip, Slam, and Plop
Solution
Marcy Schaaf
AF441090

Dedication

To my wonderful parents, Charlie and Connie Schaaf,

Thank you for turning every bump, slam, and plop into a moment of laughter and learning. Your inventive and playful solutions to life's little mishaps filled our home with joy and warmth. Your love, patience, and humor have shaped so many cherished memories, and this story is just one of many that celebrates the fun-filled lessons you taught us.

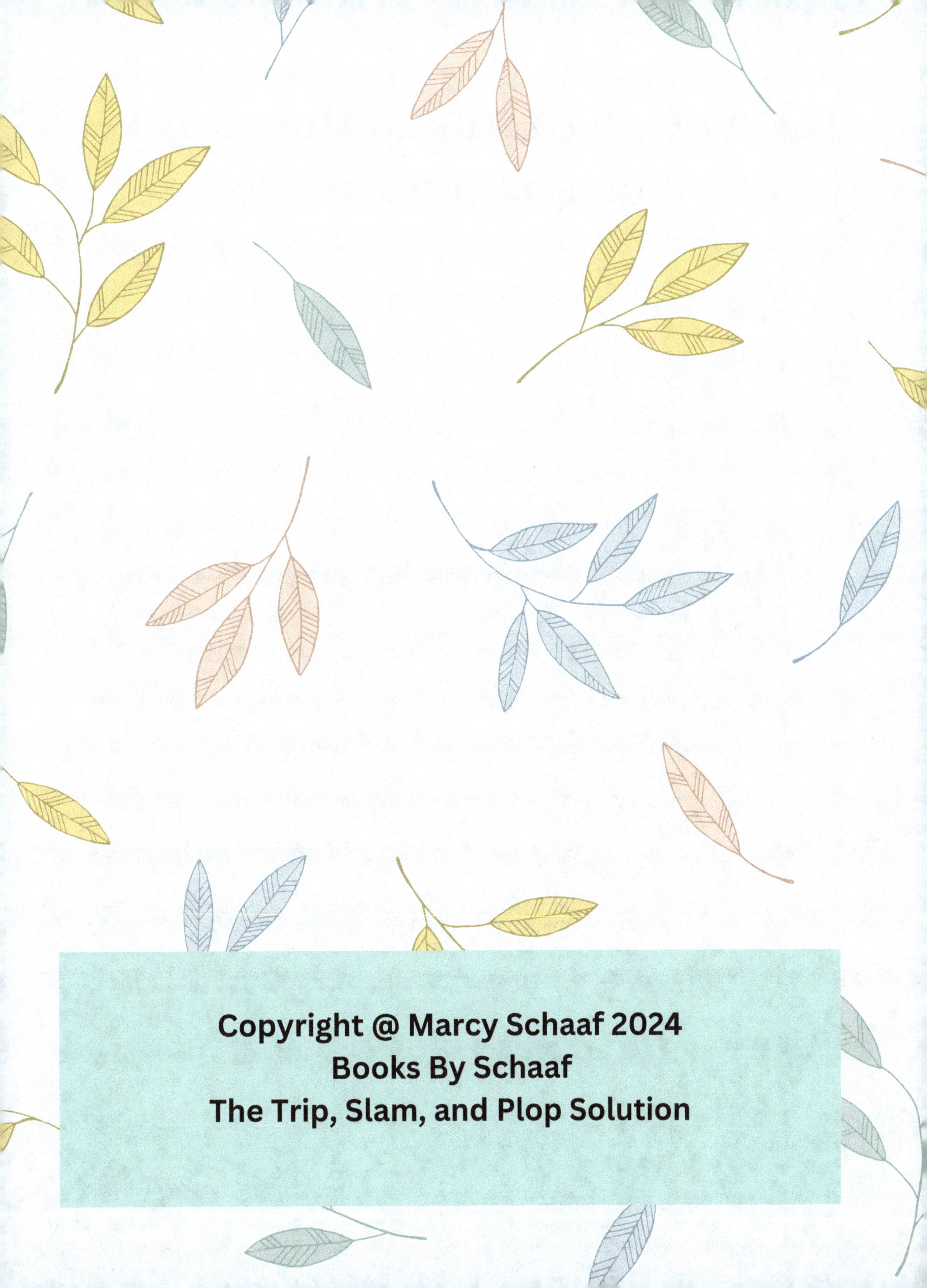

Joe loved to run up the stairs—
fast as lightning!

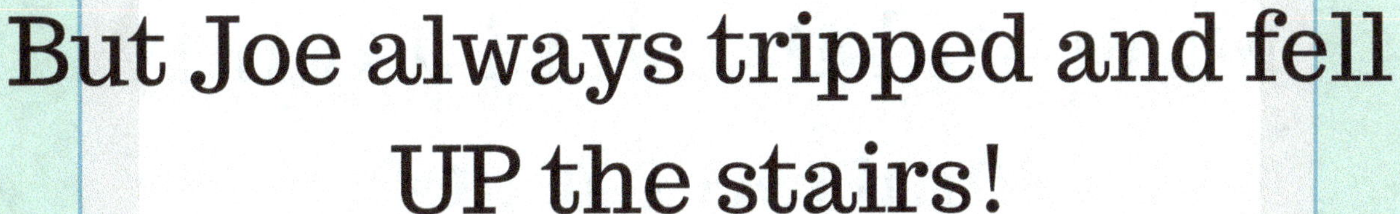

But Joe always tripped and fell
UP the stairs!

Mom and Dad had a funny
solution for Joe.

"Walk up and down the stairs 10 times, Joe!"

Joe thought it was silly, but he did it anyway.

Up and down, up and down—Joe kept walking!

He tried to go slow, but Joe still tripped!

Mom and Dad laughed and said,
"Try again, Joe!"

Joe finally made it without tripping—hooray!

Next, Joe slammed the door—
BANG!

Mom and Dad called,
"Joe, do it 10 times, please!"

Open, close, open, close—
Joe did it again.

Joe was learning to be careful
and gentle.

One day, Joe plopped on the couch—BUMP!

"Joe, stand up and sit down
10 times!" said Dad.

Joe jumped up and down, up and down!

He giggled every time he had to
do it again.

After that, Joe was careful not to plop.

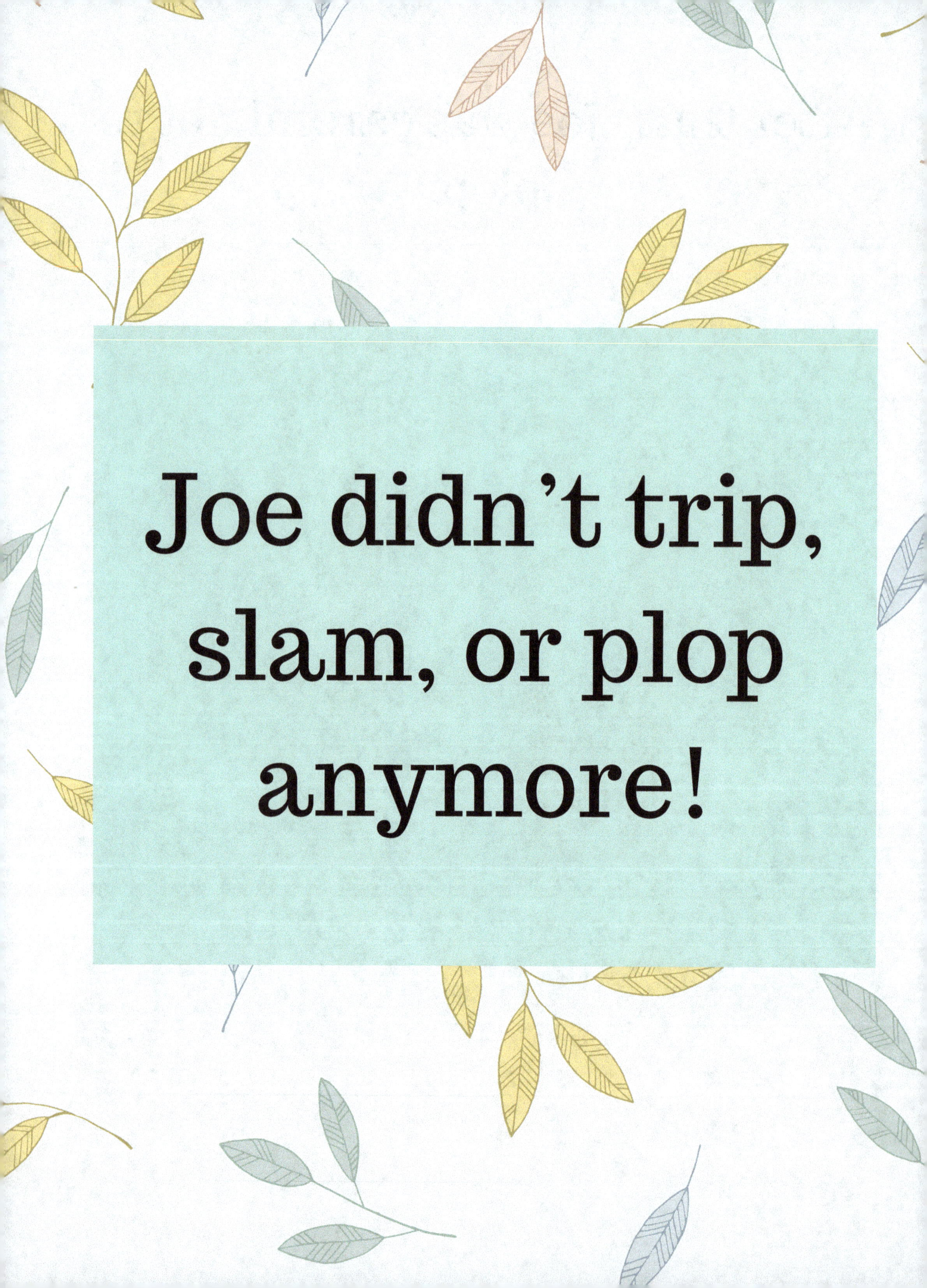
Joe didn't trip, slam, or plop anymore!

But he still loved to run up the stairs—fast!

One day, he forgot and tripped
UP again—oops!

Mom and Dad just smiled,
"You know what to do, Joe!"

Up and down, up and down—Joe walked with a grin.

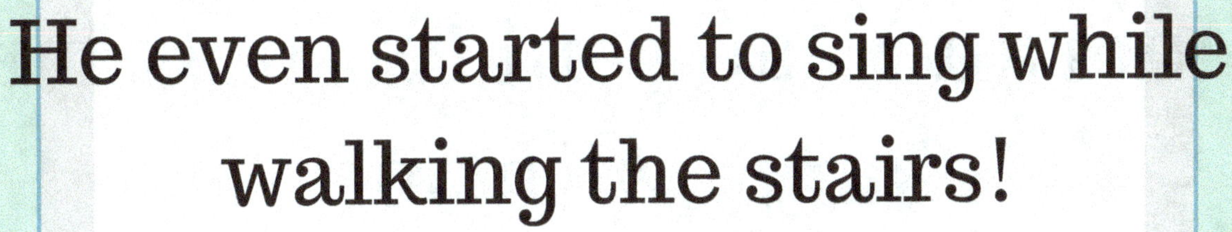

He even started to sing while walking the stairs!

Mom and Dad couldn't help but laugh with Joe.

Joe's silly trips always brought big smiles.

No matter how many times he tripped, Joe stayed happy.

And that's how Joe learned to take things slow.

But he still loved to run fast—
just not up stairs!

The End

Books By Schaaf

www.BookBySchaaf.com

find us at: